# Orange Line 6
## Standardaufgaben
Grundkurs und Erweiterungskurs

von
Bernadette Kesting

sowie
Pauline Ashworth

Ernst Klett Verlag
Stuttgart · Leipzig

# Orange Line 6 Standardaufgaben Grundkurs und Erweiterungskurs

**Autorinnen:** Bernadette Kesting, Breitenworbis; Pauline Ashworth, Stuttgart

**Zeichenerklärung:**

⊚ Übungen mit diesem Symbol verweisen auf die CD zum Hörverstehen.

**Illustrationen:** Simone Pahl, Berlin (alle, außer Seite 41: Dorothee Wolters, Köln)

**Bildquellenverzeichnis: 7.1** iStockphoto (RF/Sam Lee), Calgary, Alberta; **10.1** shutterstock (Caitlin Mirra), New York, NY; **18.1** shutterstock (Caitlin Mirra), New York, NY; **20.1** Fotolia LLC (Niceshot), New York, NY; **21.1** Ullstein Bild GmbH (iT), Berlin; **25.1** Klett-Archiv (Klett-Archiv), Stuttgart; **25.2** shutterstock (Pjasha), New York, NY; **33.1** Klett-Archiv (Klett-Archiv), Stuttgart; **33.2** shutterstock (Pjasha), New York, NY; **37.1**; **37.2** iStockphoto (s-dmit), Calgary, Alberta; **41.1** MEV Verlag GmbH (MEV, Augsburg), Augsburg; **41.2** iStockphoto (Redmal), Calgary, Alberta; **41.3** shutterstock (IKO), New York, NY; **41.4** Ingram Publishing, Tattenhall Chester; **41.5** shutterstock (Picsfive), New York, NY; **51.1** Klett-Archiv (Fabian H. Silberzahn), Stuttgart; **52.1** Fotolia LLC (Maria Fürhacker), New York; **52.2** iStockphoto (RF/Peter Clark), Calgary, Alberta; **52.3** shutterstock ( Diane Garcia), New York, NY; **52.4** shutterstock (Lance Bellers), New York, NY; **56.1** Avenue Images GmbH RF (Image Source/RF), Hamburg; **58.1**; **58.2** Thinkstock (iStockphoto), München; **59.1** Thinkstock (iStockphoto), München; **60.1**; **60.2** Thinkstock (iStockphoto), München; **60.3** Thinkstock (AbleStock.com), München; **68.1**; **68.2** Thinkstock (iStockphoto), München; **69.1**; **69.2** Thinkstock (iStockphoto), München; **70.1**; **70.2** Thinkstock (iStockphoto), München; **70.3** Thinkstock (AbleStock.com), München

Sollte es in einem Einzelfall nicht gelungen sein, den korrekten Rechteinhaber ausfindig zu machen, so werden berechtigte Ansprüche selbstverständlich im Rahmen der üblichen Regelungen abgegolten.

1. Auflage  1 $^{6\ 5\ 4\ 3\ 2\ 1}$ | 2014 2013 2012 2011 2010

Alle Drucke dieser Auflage sind unverändert und können im Unterricht nebeneinander verwendet werden. Die letzte Zahl bezeichnet das Jahr des Druckes.

Das Werk und seine Teile sind urheberrechtlich geschützt. Das Gleiche gilt für Software sowie das Begleitmaterial. Jede Nutzung in anderen als den gesetzlich zugelassenen oder in den Lizenzbestimmungen (CD) genannten Fällen bedarf der vorherigen schriftlichen Einwilligung des Verlages. Hinweis § 52 a UrhG: Weder das Werk noch seine Teile dürfen ohne eine solche Einwilligung eingescannt und in ein Netzwerk eingestellt werden. Dies gilt auch für Intranets von Schulen und sonstigen Bildungseinrichtungen. Fotomechanische oder andere Wiedergabeverfahren nur mit Genehmigung des Verlages.
© und ℗ Ernst Klett Verlag GmbH, Stuttgart 2010.
Alle Rechte vorbehalten.
www.klett.de

**Redaktion:** Lektorat editoria, Cornelia Schaller, Fellbach
**Satz und Gestaltung:** Sabine Kittel
**Umschlaggestaltung:** Koma Amok, Stuttgart
**Umschlagfoto:** Avenue Images GmbH RF (Digital Vision), Hamburg; Getty Images (fotonika/Berg), München
**Reproduktion:** Meyle + Müller, Medien-Management, Pforzheim
**Druck:** Medienhaus Plump, Rheinbreitbach

Printed in Germany
978-3-12-547564-9

**Audio-CD**

**Aufnahmeleitung:** Ernst Klett Verlag GmbH, Stuttgart
**Redaktion:** Lektorat editoria, Cornelia Schaller, Fellbach
Aufgenommen in Q Sound, London
**Aufnahme:** Tim Woolf
**Produktion:** John Green, TEFL Tapes
**Sprecherinnen und Sprecher:** Matt Addis; Harriet Carmichael; John Chancer; Melissa Collier; DeNica Fairman; Rupert Farley; Sasha de Goguel; Joanna Hall; John Hasler; Walter Lewis; Roger May; David Menkin; Rhonda Millar; Nigel Pilkington; Dominic Rowntree; Becca Stuart; Joanna Wyatt
**Tontechnik:** Tim Woolf
**Presswerk:** P+O Compact Disc, Diepholz

**Gesamtzeit:** 29'15"

## Inhalt

| | |
|---|---|
| Topic 1 GK | 4 |
| Topic 1 EK | 11 |
| Topic 2 GK | 19 |
| Topic 2 EK | 27 |
| Topic 3 GK | 35 |
| Topic 3 EK | 43 |
| Topic 4 GK | 52 |
| Topic 4 EK | 61 |
| Inhalt Audio-CD | 72 |

Die Lösungen, HV-Texte und eine Übersicht über die Aufgabentypen sowie alternative Übungen zu den Kompetenzen und zusätzliche Übungen zu Wortschatz und Grammatik finden Sie auf der hinten eingeklebten Lehrersoftware-CD.

# Topic 1  A 'global' language

## 1 Listening: Interview for a job

a) *Listen to the dialogue. Are the following statements right or wrong? Tick (✔).*

| Mr Cross advises Gemma … | right | wrong |
|---|---|---|
| 1. to buy some new trousers. | | |
| 2. to dress nicely for the interview. | | |
| 3. to find out where the company is. | | |
| 4. to find out how she gets there. | | |
| 5. to find out about the company. | | |
| 6. to be able to ask questions about the company to show interest. | | |
| 7. not to forget that the job interviewer may be very intelligent. | | |
| 8. to think about what questions the job interviewer may ask her. | | |
| 9. to talk to people who have already been to job interviews. | | |

b) *What do you think of Gemma's reactions? Tick (✔) the two correct boxes in each part (1–4).*

| Parts of the interview which Mr Cross practises with Gemma: | Gemma's answers are … | | | She is … | | |
|---|---|---|---|---|---|---|
| | much too short. | short but OK. | long enough. | clumsy and nervous. | nervous but ready to talk. | natural. |
| 1. welcome and introduction | | | | | | |
| 2. school and exams | | | | | | |
| 3. reasons why she applied | | | | | | |
| 4. how suitable she is for the job | | | | | | |

c) *What tips does Mr Cross give Gemma? Complete the sentences with the missing words.*

Mr Cross advises Gemma to find (1) _____ that describe herself.

Then Mr Cross advises Gemma to make a list of her (2) _____ and

her (3) _____ .

d) *How does Mr Cross do his job as a career's teacher? Tick (✔) the correct box.*

Mr Cross …
1. is nervous but helpful.
2. makes fun of Gemma because she is so clumsy.
3. is calm and friendly and explains well.

## 2 Reading: About the English language

You'll never visit England or the USA so you don't need English? Think again! People use English in many parts of the world and in many areas of life; science, business and the media, for example. This is because Britain played an important role globally in the 18th, 19th and 20th centuries and since the beginning of the 20th century the USA has helped to keep English important.

5 You've heard that English came from German but it doesn't sound like German? Well, in the fifth century it probably sounded like German or, at least, Old German. We call the English from that time 'Old English' and words like *ship*, *that* and *bath* come from this time. But English never stayed the same; it changed when people from different countries attacked and came to live in England and brought their own languages with them. For example, the Vikings[1] attacked England in the 9th

10 century and brought their own language with them. Words like *sky* and *leg* come from this time. Then in the 11th and 12th centuries England was attacked by the Normans[2] and a Norman, William the Conqueror, became King of England. After some time many French words came into the English language, words like *pork* and *prince*. This is one reason why there are so many words and so many synonyms in English. Some words come from the French and some from the German. For example,

15 "flower" comes from the French *fleur* and "bloom", which is also a word for a flower, comes from the German, *Blume*.

In fact every time English met another language, for example when the English attacked and lived in other countries or when England was attacked, new words came into the language. For example, shampoo came from India and *potato* from Haiti.

20 English is still changing now. Some people say that about 25,000 new words come into the English language every year, but it is difficult to say exactly because there is no official definition of English – not like for the German or French languages. Many new words come into English from other languages, for example, *kindergarten* and *kitsch* from German, or *pukka*, from Hindi. And then we need new words when new things are invented, for example, the laptop or a DVD player.

25 Not only is the vocabulary of English changing but also the spelling and the grammar. Children in English schools can usually use English or American spelling, for example. And then slang is changing all the time, too. What is *cool* one

30 year is *awesome* the next!

[1]Viking ['vaɪkɪŋ] – *Wikinger*, [2]Norman ['nɔːmən] – *Normanne*

a) *Read the text and write down (you needn't write full sentences) ...*

| | |
|---|---|
| 1. how important English is: | _____ |
| 2. how English became important: | _____ |
| 3. what languages/ people changed the English language: | _____ |

# GK 1 Reading

4. how these changes often happened:

5. how English is changing today:

6. what parts of the English language are still changing:

b) *Complete the grid with the missing facts. You needn't write full sentences.*

| time | What happened? | examples of words that go back to that time |
|---|---|---|
|  | Old English developed from old German languages |  |
|  |  |  |
|  |  |  |

Orange Line 6
ISBN 978-3-12-547564-9

c) *What sort of text is it? Tick (✔) the best box.*

The text …
1. is for scientists and experts who know a lot about language systems. ☐
2. informs us about the history of the English language in a popular way so that readers can understand it easily. ☐
3. is taken from a children's book and tells kids about the English language in a very simple and entertaining way. ☐

## 3 Writing: Your opinion

1. *Which language will be the most widely spoken in the world in 2050?*

*Answer the question. Give reasons for your opinion.*
*You may think of aspects like:*
- *if English will still be the most widely spoken and written language,*
- *what changes in the English language may take place in the future,*
- *what other languages may become more important and/or*
- *if there will even be one global language one day.*

*OR*

2. *Being a hairdresser on a cruise ship*

*Write a profile for a person who wants to apply for a job as a hairdresser on a cruise ship. What skills and strengths does he/she need?*

_____
_____
_____
_____
_____
_____
_____

## 4 Writing: An e-mail to a sponsor

*Imagine a big company in your twin town in GB is going to sponsor your football team on a one-week course.*
*For your team, send an e-mail to them and ask them:*
  - *where and when the next course will be,*
  - *about the number of team members who can join in the coaching,*
  - *about the coaching,*
  - *about the camp and the meals,*
  - *about free-time activities,*
  - *…*

*Start your e-mail with "Dear Sir/Madam …" Write in your exercise book.*

## 5 Speaking: A telephone interview for a job

Situation: Your family is moving to Lancaster in the north of England next summer because of your father's new job there. You have applied for a job at a travel company. They want to do a telephone interview with you.

| | | |
|---|---|---|
| You: | _____ | Say hello to Mr Evans from the travel company and thank him for calling you. |
| Interviewer: | You're welcome. Now. I've got your application form here. You are from Oberhof. That's in Thüringen, isn't it? | |
| You: | _____ | Tell him that that is right and that O. is a famous holiday place in Thüringen. |
| Interviewer: | Well, our company is thinking of offering walking, trekking and climbing tours in Thüringen. Therefore we're interested in an employee who knows the area and who speaks German. You're going to finish school in June. Is that right? | |
| You: | _____ | Tell him when you are going to leave school. |
| Interviewer: | What exams are you taking? | |
| You: | _____ | Tell him. |
| Interviewer: | What is your favourite subject? | |
| You: | _____ | Tell him about your favourite subject and why you like it. |
| Interviewer: | Why do you want to work for our travel company? | |
| You: | _____ | Tell him why and why you will probably like working there. |
| Interviewer: | Why do you think we should give you the job? | |
| You: | _____ | Tell him about your strengths and why the job may be the right one for you. |
| Interviewer: | Thanks a lot for your answers. Just one final thing. We usually ask applicants to fill in a profile form. I'll send it to you. Could you send it back as soon as possible, please. | |
| You: | _____ | Tell him that you will do that. |

## 6 Writing/Speaking: Your turn

1. *The profile form that Mr Evans sent you is below. Complete it.*

Name: _____

| Education: | _____ |
| Job experience: | _____ |
| | _____ |
| | _____ |
| Skills: | _____ |
| Strengths: | _____ |
| | _____ |
| | _____ |
| Weaknesses: | _____ |
| Family: | _____ |
| | _____ |
| My dream: | _____ |
| | _____ |
| In the next 12 month: | _____ |
| | _____ |
| Interesting info: | _____ |
| | _____ |

OR

2. *A talk about yourself*

In a job interview you are often asked to introduce yourself *(dich selbst vorstellen)* and to give a short talk about yourself. They are interested in the following aspects:
- family,
- education and qualifications,
- job/work experience,
- skills,
- strengths and weaknesses,
- your dream(s) for your career and future life,
- how you hope your life and career will develop in the next 12 months,
- hobbies and other interesting things about you.

*Make notes in your exercise book on what you are going to say.*

## 7 Mediation: The official language in the US

Situation: Du hast irgendwo gehört, dass die deutsche Sprache nach Gründung der USA beinahe zur Landessprache dort geworden wäre und dass mit nur einer Stimme Mehrheit die Entscheidung zugunsten von Englisch ausfiel. Du findest im Internet einen Artikel, der sagt, dass es sich dabei um eine Legende handelt.

**German the official US language?**
**Did German lose against English by just one vote?**

The legend usually goes something like this: In 1776, English won over German by just one vote and English
5   became America's official language instead of[1] German. It is a story that Germans, German teachers and many other people like to tell. But is it true?

Germans have always played an important role in US history. But a closer look shows several serious[2]
10   problems with this "official language" story. First of all the United States has never had an "official language" – English, German or any other – and doesn't have one now. And there was never a vote like this in 1776.

*Independence Hall in Philadelphia, Pennsylvania*

In 1795 US Congress discussed languages and a vote about German probably took place in 1795, but this vote
15   dealt with[3] translating[4] US laws into German. A few months later, however, the idea of translating laws into languages other than English was dropped.
It is likely that the legend of German as the official language of the US started in the 1930s. Scientists think that the legend was part of the German-American Bund propaganda spread by the Nazis. They wanted to give the German language more weight and importance in the world. By mixing this wish with historical events in
20   Pennsylvania, the German-American Bund probably produced this "national vote" story.

[1]instead of [ɪnˈsted ˌəv] – *statt*, [2]serious [ˈsɪərɪəs] – *ernst(haft)*,
[3]to deal with [ˈdiːl wɪð] – *sich drehen um*, [4]to translate [trænzˈleɪt] – *übersetzen*

1. Nenne die zwei Hauptargumente, die beweisen, dass es sich um eine Legende handelt.

2. Auf welchen tatsächlichen historischen Begebenheiten könnte die Legende basieren?

3. Welche Ereignisse nach 1930 trugen möglicherweise zur Entstehung und Verbreitung der Legende bei?

# Topic 1  A 'global' language

## 1 Listening: Interview for a job

a) *Listen to the dialogue. Are the following statements right or wrong? Tick (✔).*

| Mr Cross advises Gemma … | right | wrong |
|---|---|---|
| 1. to buy some new trousers. | | |
| 2. to dress nicely for the interview. | | |
| 3. to find out where the company is. | | |
| 4. to find out how she gets there. | | |
| 5. to find out about the company. | | |
| 6. to be able to ask questions about the company to show interest. | | |
| 7. not to forget that the job interviewer may be very intelligent. | | |
| 8. to think about what questions the job interviewer may ask her. | | |
| 9. to be prepared to give answers which show that she is confident. | | |
| 10. to practise for the interview in front of a mirror. | | |

b) *What do you think of Gemma's reactions? Tick (✔) the two correct boxes in each part (1–4).*

| Parts of the interview which Mr Cross practises with Gemma: | Gemma's answers are … | | | She seems to be … | | |
|---|---|---|---|---|---|---|
| | much too short. | short but OK. | long enough and good. | clumsy and nervous. | nervous but ready to talk. | natural and confident. |
| 1. welcome and introduction | | | | | | |
| 2. school and exams | | | | | | |
| 3. reasons why she applied | | | | | | |
| 4. how suitable she is for the job | | | | | | |

c) *What tips does Mr Cross give Gemma? Complete the sentences with the missing words.*

Mr Cross advises Gemma to answer with (1) _____ to tell the

job interviewer (2) _____ she is and how well she has prepared for her

(3) _____. Then Mr Cross advises Gemma not only to mention that a job at an

insurance company is (4) _____ but also to show

that she would find (5) _____.

d) *How does Mr Cross do his job as a career's teacher? Tick (✔) the correct box.*

Mr Cross …
1. is nervous but understanding and helpful. ☐
2. makes fun of Gemma because she is so clumsy. ☐
3. stays calm and friendly and explains well. ☐

## 2 Reading: About the English language

English is a lingua franca in many parts of the world and in many areas of life; science, business and the media, for example. This is because Britain played an important role globally in the 18th, 19th and 20th century, and since the beginning of the 20th century the USA has helped to keep English important.

5 But how did the English language develop? It started in the fifth century when settlers came to England from Northern Europe. 'Old English', as it is now called, developed from their language. Words like *ship*, *that* and *bath* come from this time. English never stayed the same, though; it changed as people from different countries attacked and came to live in England and brought their own language, Norse[1], with them. For example, the Vikings[2] attacked England in the 9th
10 century and brought their own language with them. Words like *sky* and *leg* come from this time. The biggest change, though, happened in the 11th and 12th centuries when England was attacked by the Normans[3] and after the Norman Conquest a Norman, William the Conqueror, became King of England. At first the richer and more powerful people spoke French and the rest spoke English. Then, after some time, things began to change and many French words came into the English language.
15 10,000 French (or Norman) words came into the English language at this time, e.g. *prison* and *prince*. This is one reason why there are so many words and so many synonyms in English. Some words with the same or a similar meaning have a German origin and some have a French origin. For example, *flower* comes from the French *fleur* and *bloom*, which is also a word for a flower, comes from the German *Blume*. Most English words came from other languages but there are many words that were
20 made up. Shakespeare made up lots of new words (sometimes from other words) or used old words for new things. For example, Shakespeare gave us the words, *lonely*, *hurry* and *excellent*. And we have no idea where some words, like *dog* and *fun*, came from.
Every time English has met another language, in England or abroad, for example, when the English attacked and lived in other countries, or during World War I and II, new words came into the
25 language. For example, *shampoo* came from India from a Hindi word, *potato* from Haitian, and *slogan* from Gaelic. Many Latin[4] and Greek words came into English, too, but most of them came via a different language and often the meaning changed, along the way. For example, the words *disk*, *dish*[5] and *desk* all come from the Latin word "discus" but they came into the English language at different times and in different ways.
30 English is still changing today. Some people say that about 25,000 new words come into the English language every year, but it is difficult to say exactly how many because there is no official definition of English – unlike for the German or French languages. Many new words come into English from other languages, for example, *kindergarten* and *kitsch* from German. And then we need new words when new things are invented, for example, the laptop, or a DVD player.
35 Not only is the vocabulary of English changing but also the grammar, and we are also getting new expressions. Sometimes these expressions come from different types of slang. Many groups of people have their own slang. One famous type of slang is Cockney rhyming slang which comes from East London. They use expressions which rhyme with a word, for example, *'loaf of bread*[6]*'* means head. So if somebody says, "Use your loaf", they mean "use your *head*" or "think".

[1]Norse [nɔːs] – *Altnordisch*, [2]Viking [ˈvaɪkɪŋ] – *Wikinger*, [3]Norman [ˈnɔːmən] – *Normanne*, [4]Latin [ˈlætn] – *Latein*, [5]dish [dɪʃ] – *Gericht (Essen)*, [6]loaf of bread [ˌləʊf əv ˈbred] – *Brotlaib*

Reading 1 EK

a) Complete the mind map with the missing information.

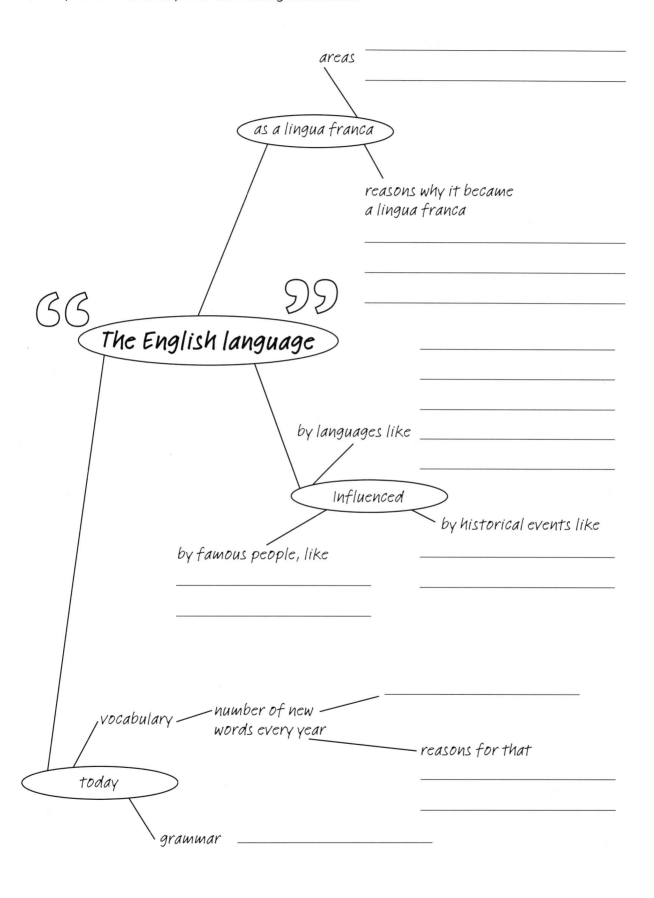

**EK 1** | Reading

b) *Complete the grid with the missing facts. You needn't write full sentences.*

| time | What happened?/ What influenced the English language? | examples of words that go back to that time |
|---|---|---|
|  | Settlers from Northern Europe, Old English developed |  |
|  |  |  |
|  |  |  |
|  |  |  |

c) *Explain why the English language is so rich in words and why there are so many synonyms.*

_____

_____

_____

_____

_____

d) *What sort of text is it? Tick (✔) the best box.*

The text …
1. has a scientific character and explains the influence of other languages on English in great detail. ☐
2. informs us about the history of the English language in a popular way so that readers can understand it easily. ☐
3. seems to be taken from a children's book and tells kids about the changes in the English language in a very simple and entertaining way. ☐

## 3 Writing: Your opinion

1. *Which language will be the most widespread language in the world in 2050?*
*Answer the question. Give reasons for your opinion.*
*You may think of aspects like:*
   - whether English will still be the most widely spoken and written language,
   - what changes in the English language may take place in the future,
   - what other languages may become important and/or
   - if there will even be one global language one day.

OR

2. *Bilingual lessons*
More and more schools in Germany teach bilingually. And not only traditional subjects like Geography or History are taught in English or French, also Art or PE.
Would you like to have bilingual sports lessons, too?
*Write a text and answer the question. Think of the advantages and disadvantages.*
*Give reasons for your opinion.*

_____
_____
_____
_____
_____
_____
_____
_____
_____
_____

## 4 Speaking: A telephone interview for a job

Situation: Your family is moving to Lancaster in the north of England next summer because of your father's new job there. You have applied for a job at a travel company. They have offered you the opportunity to do a telephone interview.

| | | |
|---|---|---|
| You: | _____ | *Begrüße deinen Gesprächspartner Mr Evans und bedanke dich für die Gelegenheit, mit ihm telefonieren zu können.* |
| Interviewer: | You're welcome. Now. I've got your application form here. You are from Oberhof. That's in Thuringia, isn't it? | |
| You: | _____ | *Bejahe und sage, dass es ein beliebter Ferienort in Thüringen ist.* |

| | | |
|---|---|---|
| Interviewer: | Well, our company is thinking of offering walking, trekking and climbing tours in Thuringia. Therefore we're interested in an employee who knows the area and who speaks German. You're going to finish school in June. Is that right? | |
| You: | _____ _____ | *Erkläre, wann du die Schule verlassen wirst und mit welchem Schulabschluss.* |
| Interviewer: | Which written and oral school leaving exams will you be taking? | |
| You: | _____ _____ | *Sage, welche schriftlichen und mündlichen Abschlussprüfungen du ablegen wirst.* |
| Interviewer: | And are you confident you'll pass your exams? | |
| You: | _____ _____ _____ _____ | *Stelle dar, wie du dich auf die Abschlussprüfungen vorbereitest und mit welchem Ziel.* |
| Interviewer: | And can you tell me what your favourite subject is. | |
| You: | _____ _____ | *Antworte ausführlich.* |
| Interviewer: | Why do you want to work for our travel company? | |
| You: | _____ _____ _____ | *Begründe ausführlich.* |
| Interviewer: | And can you tell me: why do you think we should give you the job? | |
| You: | _____ _____ _____ | *Begründe ausführlich.* |
| Interviewer: | Thanks a lot for your answers. Just one final question. We usually ask applicants to fill in a profile form. I'll send it to you. Could you send it back as soon as possible, please. | |
| You: | _____ _____ | *Sage zu.* |

## 5 Writing/Speaking: Your turn

1. *The profile form that Mr Evans sent you is below. Complete it.*

Name: _____

| Education: | _____ |
| Job experience: | _____ |
| Present position: | _____ |
| Special skills: | _____ |
| Personality: | _____ |
| Strengths: | _____ |
| Weaknesses: | _____ |
| Family: | _____ |
| My dream: | _____ |
| One more thing I would like people to know about me: | _____ |

OR

2. *A talk about yourself*

In a job interview the interviewers ask you to introduce yourself and to give a short talk about yourself. They are interested in the following aspects:
- family,
- education and qualifications,
- job/work experience,
- present position,
- special skills and qualifications,
- personality, strengths and weaknesses,
- your dream(s) for your career and future life,
- how you hope your life and career will develop in the next 12 months,
- hobbies and one or more things you would like people to know about you.

*Make notes in your exercise book on what you are going to say.*

## 6 Mediation: The official language in the US

Situation: Du hast irgendwo gehört, dass die deutsche Sprache nach Gründung der USA beinahe zur Landessprache dort geworden wäre und dass mit nur einer Stimme Mehrheit die Entscheidung zugunsten von Englisch ausfiel. Du findest im Internet einen Artikel, der sagt, dass es sich dabei um eine Legende handelt.

**German the official US language?**
**Did German lose against English by just one vote?**

The legend usually goes something like this: In 1776, English won over German by just one vote and English became America's official language instead of German. It is a story that Germans, German teachers and many other people like to tell. But is it true?

At first sight it may sound possible. Germans have always played an important role in US history. But a closer look shows several serious problems with this "official language" story. First of all the United States has never had an "official language" – English, German or any other – and doesn't have one now. And there was never any such vote in 1776.

In 1795 US Congress debated[1] on languages and a vote on German probably took place in 1795, but this vote dealt with[2] translating US laws into German. A few months later, however[3], the idea of publishing laws in languages other than English was dropped.
It is likely that the legend of German as the official language of the US started in the 1930s. Scientists think that the legend was part of the German-American Bund propaganda spread by the Nazis and aimed at[4] giving the German language more weight and importance in the world. By mixing this wish with certain historical events in Pennsylvania, the German-American Bund probably produced this "national vote" story.

*Independence Hall in Philadelphia, Pennsylvania*

[1]to debate [dɪˈbeɪt] – *debattieren*, [2]to deal with [ˈdiːl wɪð] – *sich drehen um*,
[3]however [haʊˈevə] – *jedoch*, [4]to aim at [eɪm] – *abzielen auf*

1. Nenne die zwei Hauptargumente, die beweisen, dass es sich um eine Legende handelt.

2. Auf welchen tatsächlichen historischen Begebenheiten könnte die Legende basieren?

3. Welche Ereignisse nach 1930 trugen möglicherweise zur Entstehung und Verbreitung der Legende bei?

# Topic 2  Living democracy – human rights

## 1 Listening: Talking about work experience[1]

a) *Listen and tick (✔) the right box.*

| Who … | Kyle | Emma | guy from music dept. |
|---|---|---|---|
| 1. is doing work experience for a big department store? | | | |
| 2. meets sb in a café after work on Friday? | | | |
| 3. is totally happy working for the department store? | | | |
| 4. was bored by the work he/she/they did? | | | |
| 5. worked in the music department? | | | |
| 6. should not stand so near to someone else? | | | |
| 7. has a problem with asking someone to respect his/her/their personal space? | | | |
| 8. is very strict about respecting the personal space of others? | | | |

[1]work experience ['wɜːk ɪkˌspɪərɪəns] – *Praktikum*

b) *Find the missing words and complete the text.*

Emma thinks that just standing (1) _____ or touching her may not be

an act of harassing. It may just be (2) _____.

Kyle advises her to talk to her (3) _____, but Emma does not like that

idea. She is worried that she would never get (4) _____ at the department

store then. Emma thinks that it is more (5) _____ for girls.

c) *Tick (✔) the two correct boxes.*

Kyle wishes that Liz from the sports department would **not** …
1. make embarrassing jokes when he is around or even touch him.
2. treat him like a teenager.
3. treat him like a jerk or like someone who is a bit clumsy.
4. treat him like a buddy or like a colleague she has known for a long time.

d) *Which sentence shows Kyle's and Emma's problem best? Tick (✔) the correct box.*

Both Kyle and Emma …
1. think that they should talk to their supervisors.
2. think that they should try to live with embarrassing situations like sexist jokes.
3. do not dare to talk openly to Liz or the other guy about their feelings.

## 2 Reading: Queen of the United Kingdom, Canada, Australia, New Zealand and many more

Queen Elizabeth II is, as most people know, Queen of England but, as many people don't know, she is also Queen of the United Kingdom (England, Scotland, Wales and Northern Ireland) and Queen of 15 other countries including Canada, Australia, New Zealand and Tuvalu. What does that mean? What powers does she have? And where are these countries?

5 In Great Britain she is the Head of State and that means she has to open Parliament, pass laws, and sign treaties with other nations. These are important things but she cannot really refuse to do them. The Queen has no real power in Great Britain. But what about in the other countries?

In Australia the Queen is called Queen of Australia. She is the official Head of State but in reality this job is done for her by the Governor-General[1] of Australia. The Queen's main duty is to appoint 10 the Governor-General (and the Governors of all the States) but she does not choose them. Just as in Great Britain the Queen opens Parliament and reads a speech which is written by the Government. The speech says what the Government wants to do that year. Again the Queen has no real power but she and members of the Royal Family visit Australia for important events, for example to open the Olympics or on Australia Day. So what do Australians think of all this? As you could expect some 15 Australians like it and some do not. In 1999 there was a vote. Australians had to vote for or against the Queen and the Royal Family. It was close! Just over 54% voted for the Queen.

Canada has a similar system to Australia. There is also a Governor-General who does most of the Queen's duties. The Queen and the Royal family also visit regularly and have houses or palaces in Canada where they stay. Usually the Queen's visits to Canada are very popular and people do not 20 argue about the monarchy in Canada as much as in Australia. In fact one survey said that many Canadians do not even know that Queen Elizabeth II is their Head of State. And what about the other countries? Most of the countries are in the Caribbean[2] and in the Pacific Ocean[3] near Australia. Tuvalu for example is a group of very small islands between Australia and Hawaii. Only about 12,000 people live there and the Queen has only visited once – in 1982. Her job there is very similar to her 25 job in Australia and Canada.

[1]Governor-General [ˌgʌvnəˈdʒenrl] – *Generalgouverneur*, [2]Caribbean [ˌkærɪˈbiːən] – *Karibik*, [3]Pacific Ocean [pəˌsɪfɪk ˈəʊʃn] – *Pazifischer Ozean*

a) *Complete the diagram with the missing facts. Find a suitable heading.*

_____

QUEEN

of: _____

_____

HEAD OF STATE

of: _____

duties/tasks:

- _____

   _____

- _____

   _____

- _____

   _____

of: _____

job is done by:

_____

duties/tasks:

_____

_____

visits:

- _____

   _____

- _____

   _____

of: *Canada*

job is done by:

_____

visits:

- _____

   _____

- _____

   _____

b) *Queen Elizabeth II does not have "real" power in Great Britain and in Australia. Find one example for each country in the text which shows this.*

_____
_____
_____
_____
_____
_____
_____

c) *What do the Australian and Canadian people think of the Queen?*

___

___

___

## 3 Writing: A story from the Middle Ages

*Look at the picture story. Complete the discussion between Friar Tuck, Robin Hood and Little John.*

1. *Sprich für Friar Tuck.*
   - Fordere die Männer auf aufzuhören (mit dem Streiten).
   - Frage sie, ob sie Ideen haben, wie ihr gegen den Sheriff von Nottingham kämpfen werdet.

   _____ arguing! Do you have any ideas _____ _____ the Sheriff of Nottingham?

2. *Sprich für Robin Hood.*
   - Grüße die Männer.
   - Sage, dass du ihnen helfen möchtest.

   _____, I'm Lord Robin of Locksley. _____ _____.

3. *Sprich für Little John.*
   - Fordere Robin auf zu beweisen, dass er Lord Robin ist.

   _____ that you are Lord Robin.

4. *Sprich für Robin Hood.*
   - Sage, dass du loyal bist dem König gegenüber und dass du für ihn kämpfen wirst.
   - Erkläre ihnen, dass der Sheriff den Tod deines Vaters verursacht und dein Land und dein Geld gestohlen hat.

   I'm _____ to the king and _____ _____ him. The Sheriff _____ my father's death and _____.

5. *Sprich für Little John.*
   - Schlage vor, Lord Robin zu testen.
   - Fordere die anderen auf, dir den großen Bogen und einen Pfeil zu bringen.
   - Sage, dass es nur einen Mann gibt, der die Kraft hat, den Bogen zu benutzen.

   _____ Lord Robin. _____ the big bow and an arrow. _____ who has the strength _____.

# Writing 2 GK

6. *Sprich für Little John.*
   - Äußere dich erfreut, dass er tatsächlich Lord Robin ist.

My goodness, _____
_____.

7. *Sprich für Robin Hood.*
   - Sage, dass der Sheriff von Nottingham Lady Marion als Geisel genommen hat.
   - Frage, was ihr tun könnt, damit der Sheriff Lady Marion freilässt.

The Sheriff of Nottingham _____
_____
hostage. _____
_____ so that the Sheriff _____
_____?

8. *Sprich für Friar Tuck.*
   - Sage, dass du eine Idee hast.
   - Sage, dass der Bischof von Hereford auf dem Weg nach Nottingham ist und durch den Sherwood Forest kommen wird.
   - Schlage vor, den Bischof zu kidnappen.

_____.

The Bishop of Hereford is on his way to Nottingham. _____
_____
Sherwood Forest. _____
_____.

## 4 Writing: Telling a story

*Tell the story of how Robin Hood and his men (Little John, Will Scarlet, Friar Tuck and others) made the Sheriff of Nottingham set Lady Marion free. Look at the letter and at the beginning.*

> To the Sheriff of Nottingham
>
> Sir,
>
> We have taken the Bishop of Hereford hostage and we have got the gold and the jewels that the bishop wanted to bring you.
>
> The bishop should have known better than to ride through Sherwood Forest after dark. It was child's play for us to attack his coach and to take him and his men prisoner.
>
> The bishop is asking you to do what we want. He promises to give you whatever you want once he is free again.
>
> We want you to set Lady Marion free!
>
> The exchange of prisoners will take place at the big city gate on Sunday at dawn.
>
> If you hurt Lady Marion, you will never get your gold and jewels back and will never see the bishop alive again.
>
> NO TRICKS!      Robin of Locksley

Robin Hood and his friends hid behind the bushes.
After some time they heard _____

## 5 Writing: Tips for young apprentices

Your class is preparing tips about what young apprentices can do in difficult or embarrassing situations.

*Advise young apprentices what to do in the following situations. Write two sentences or more for each situation.*

1. Someone you work with makes nasty comments about your looks, your religion and your family background.

2. A colleague of the opposite sex shows interest in you. He/She makes jokes and often stands too near you or even touches you.

## 6 Speaking: The duties of the Queen

*Choose a day in the Queen's life and describe it.*
*What duties does she have to do on this day? Who does she meet? Where does she go?*
*Write notes first.*

**Notes**

## 7 Mediation: Hong Kong – a former[1] British colony

On June 30, 1997 Hong Kong was given back to China after more than 150 years of being a British colony.

In 1984 Britain and the People's Republic of China signed a treaty about when and how Hong Kong should be returned[2] to its motherland.
Socialist China wanted to send its soldiers to the region, but allowed Hong Kong to keep its democratic system and capitalist market economy for 50 years. There would be "one nation, two systems".

*The flag of Hong Kong till 1997*

Since the 1960s Hong Kong has been one of the leading[3] trading[4] economies in the world and has earned more per head than Britain. The secret[5] of its success is its closeness to China and strong links with the West. Although China is Hong Kong's most important trading partner, the low taxes and the English Law system have attracted investors from all over the world for a long time. In the 1990s Hong Kong developed into a leading financial centre and became one of the richest places in the world.

They were lucky that giving back Hong Kong to socialist China in 1997 did not stop that development. Today, after years of Chinese control over Hong Kong, the people there call their political system a 'birdcage democracy'. They want back the freedom they had when Hong Kong was still a British colony.

[1]former ['fɔːmə] – *ehemalig*, [2]to return [rɪ'tɜːn] – *zurückgeben*,
[3]leading ['liːdɪŋ] – *führend*, [4]trading ['treɪdɪŋ] – *Handels-*, [5]secret ['siːkrət] – *Geheimnis*

## Mediation

a) *Bearbeite die Aufgaben.*

1. *In welcher Bedeutung werden folgende Begriffe verwendet? Markiere die richtige Bedeutung.*

| **economy** [ɪˈkɒnəmi] *Substantiv* (line 7) |
|---|
| 1. Sparsamkeit, Wirtschaftlichkeit; ☐ |
| 2. a) Sparmaßnahme, b) Einsparung; ☐ |
| 3. Wirtschaft (-ssystem *oder* -slehre) ☐ |

| **tax** [tæks] *Substantiv* (line 12) |
|---|
| 1. (Staats-)Steuer; *tax on land* Grundsteuer; ☐ |
| 2. Taxe, Gebühr; ☐ |
| 3. *übertragen* a) Bürde, Last, b) Belastung ☐ |

2. *Erschließe die Wortart von „closeness" (l. 10) und „development" (l. 16) und die deutsche Bedeutung der Begriffe.*

b) *Finde die Informationen im Text und übertrage sie ins Deutsche. Du musst keine ganzen Sätze schreiben.*

1. der politische Status von Hong Kong einst und jetzt:

2. die Forderungen und Zugeständnisse Chinas bei der Vertragsaushandlung:

3. Hong Kongs wirtschaftlicher Erfolg und die Gründe dafür:

4. die Einstellung der Menschen in Hong Kong zu ihrer Regierung:

# Topic 2  Living democracy – human rights

## 1 Listening: Talking about work experience[1]

a) *Listen and tick (✔) the right box.*

| Who ... | Kyle | Emma | journalist Rob | people at meeting |
|---|---|---|---|---|
| 1. is doing work experience for a big newspaper? | | | | |
| 2. meets sb in a café after work on Friday? | | | | |
| 3. is totally happy working for the newspaper? | | | | |
| 4. was bored by the event he/she/they went to? | | | | |
| 5. had a long discussion about matters of public interest? | | | | |
| 6. talked about collecting rubbish in parks? | | | | |
| 7. interviewed some people at the event he/she/they went to? | | | | |
| 8. should show more respect for the personal space of others? | | | | |
| 9. has a problem asking someone to respect his/her/their personal space? | | | | |
| 10. has a very strict opinion about respecting the personal space of others? | | | | |

[1] work experience ['wɜːk ɪkˌspɪərɪəns] – *Praktikum*

b) *Find the missing words and complete the text.*

Emma thinks that just standing (1) _____ or touching her may not be

harassment. It may just be (2) _____.

Kyle advises her to talk to her (3) _____, but Emma does not like

that idea. She is worried that she would (4) _____ at the

newspaper then.

Emma thinks that it is (5) _____ for girls to escape

harassment and that boys don't have the (6) _____ of harassment.

c) *Tick (✔) the two correct boxes.*

Kyle wishes that Liz, the sports reporter, would **not** ...
1. make embarrassing or sexist jokes when he is around.
2. treat him like a teenager.
3. treat him like a jerk or as someone who is a bit clumsy.
4. treat him like a buddy or like a colleague she has known for a long time.
5. provoke him to make jokes or horseplay.

d) *Which sentence shows Kyle's and Emma's attitude best? Tick (✔) the correct box.*

Both Kyle and Emma …
1. think that they should talk to their supervisors.
2. think that they should try to live with embarrassing situations like sexist jokes.
3. do not dare to talk openly to Liz or Rob about their feelings.

## 2 Reading: Queen of the United Kingdom, Canada, Australia, New Zealand and many more

Queen Elizabeth II is, as most people know, Queen of England but, as many people don't know, she is also Queen of the United Kingdom (England, Scotland, Wales and Northern Ireland) and Queen of 15 other Commonwealth countries: Australia, New Zealand, Canada, Jamaica, the Bahamas, Barbados, Grenada, St Christopher and Nevis, St Lucia, the Solomon Islands, Tuvalu, St Vincent and
5 the Grenadines, Papua New Guinea, Antigua and Barbuda and Belize. What does that mean? And what powers does she have? And where are these countries anyway?
In Great Britain she is the Head of State and she has to open and dissolve Parliament, pass laws, and sign treaties with other nations. Theoretically[1] she could refuse to do these things but practically she cannot. The Queen has no real power in Great Britain. But what about in the other countries? How do
10 Australians feel about the fact that their Head of State is the Queen of England?
In Australia the Queen is called Queen of Australia. She is officially the Head of State but actually this job is done for her by the Governor-General[2] of Australia. The Queen's main duty is to appoint the Governor-General (and the Governors of all the States) but she does not choose them. The Prime Minister chooses the Governor-General and the States choose the Governors and then advise the
15 Queen. The Queen then appoints the Governors officially. The Australian Parliament has three parts: the Queen, the Senate and the House of Representatives. At the Opening of Parliament, the Queen or the Governor-General read "The Speech from the Throne". This speech is written by the government, as in Great Britain, and says what the Government plans to do that year. Theoretically the Queen has the power to stop laws in Australia but actually she would not be allowed to do this. The Queen or
20 members of the Royal Family visit Australia quite often for important events, for example to open the Olympics or on Australia Day. The Queen has visited 15 times up to now. So what do Australians think of all this? As you would expect some Australians like it and some do not. In 1999 there was a vote. Australians had to vote for or against the Queen and the Royal Family. It was close! Just over 54% voted for the Queen.
25 Canada has a similar system to Australia. There is also a Governor-General who does most of the Queen's duties. The Queen and the Royal family also visit regularly and have houses or palaces in Canada where they stay. Usually the Queen's visits to Canada are very popular and there is not as much discussion about the monarchy in Canada as there is in Australia. In fact many Canadians do not even know that Queen Elizabeth II is their Head of State. Most of the people in Canada who are
30 against the monarch live in Quebec, the French-speaking part of Canada.
And what about the other countries? Most of the countries are in the Caribbean[3] and in the Pacific Ocean[4] near Australia. Tuvalu for example is a group of very small islands between Australia and Hawaii. Only about 12,000 people live there and the Queen has only visited once – in 1982. Her job there is very similar to her job in Australia and Canada.

[1]theoretically [ˌθɪəˈretɪkli] – *theoretisch*, [2]Governor-General [ˌɡʌvnəˈdʒenrl] – *Generalgouverneur*,
[3]Caribbean [ˌkærɪˈbiːən] – *Karibik*, [4]Pacific Ocean [pəˌsɪfɪk ˈəʊʃn] – *Pazifischer Ozean*

a) *Complete the diagram with the missing facts. Find a suitable heading.*

_____

QUEEN

of: _____

_____

HEAD OF STATE

| of: _____ | of: _____ | of: *Canada* |
|---|---|---|
| duties/tasks: | job is done by: | job is done by: |
| • _____ | _____ | _____ |
| _____ | duties/tasks: | visits: |
| • _____ | _____ | • _____ |
| _____ | _____ | _____ |
| • _____ | at opening of Parliament: | • _____ |
| _____ | _____ | |
| at opening of Parliament: | _____ | |
| _____ | visits: | |
| _____ | • _____ | |
| | _____ | |
| | • _____ | |
| | _____ | |

b) *Explain what powers Queen Elizabeth II has in Great Britain and in Australia.*

_____

_____

_____

_____

c) *Compare the attitude of the Australian population towards the Queen to the attitude the Canadians have.*

## 3 Writing: A story from the Middle Ages

*Look at the picture story. Complete the discussion between Friar Tuck, Robin Hood and Little John.*

1. *Sprich für Friar Tuck.*
   - Fordere die Männer auf aufzuhören (mit dem Streiten).
   - Frage sie, wie ihr jemals gegen den Sheriff von Nottingham kämpfen wollt, wenn ihr streitet.
   - Sagen ihnen, was ihr braucht, ist ein guter Anführer.

2. *Sprich für Robin Hood.*
   - Sprich die Männer an.
   - Stelle dich vor als Lord Robin of Locksley.
   - Sage, dass du ihnen helfen möchtest.

3. *Sprich für Little John.*
   - Fordere Robin auf zu beweisen, dass er Lord Robin ist.

4. *Sprich für Robin Hood.*
   - Sage den Männern, dass du loyal bist dem König gegenüber und dass du für ihn kämpfen wirst.
   - Erkläre ihnen, dass der Sheriff von Nottingham den Tod deines Vaters verursacht und dein Land und dein Geld gestohlen hat.

5. *Sprich für Little John.*
   - Schlage vor, Lord Robin zu testen.
   - Fordere die anderen auf, dir den großen Bogen und einen Pfeil zu bringen.
   - Sage, dass es nur einen Mann gibt, der die Kraft hat, den Bogen zu benutzen.

6. *Sprich für Little John.*
   - Äußere dich erfreut, dass es tatsächlich Lord Robin ist.

7. *Sprich für Robin Hood.*
   - Sage, dass der Sheriff von Nottingham Lady Marion als Geisel genommen hat.
   - Frage, wie ihr den Sheriff zwingen könnt, Lady Marion frei zu lassen.

8. *Sprich für Friar Tuck.*
   - Sage, dass der Bischof von Hereford auf dem Weg nach Nottingham ist und durch den Sherwood Forest kommen wird.
   - Schlage vor, den Bischof zu kidnappen.

## 4 Writing: Telling a story

*Tell the story of how Robin Hood and his men (Little John, Will Scarlet, Friar Tuck and others) made the Sheriff of Nottingham set Lady Marion free. Look at the clues and at the beginning.*

| people | | |
|---|---|---|
| Robin Hood | Friar Tuck | Will Scarlet |
| Little John | LADY MARION | other men |
| Bishop of Heresford | coachman, body guards | Sheriff of Nottingham |
| **places** | | |
| Sherwood Forest | headquarters | trees and bushes |
| bags of gold | NOTTINGHAM CASTLE | prison |
| coach | ride through Sherwood Forest | city of Nottingham |

*Robin Hood and his friends hid behind the bushes. After some time they heard the Bishop's coach.*

| actions | | |
|---|---|---|
| attack | fight with bows and arrows | catch |
| take prisoner | TAKE HOSTAGE | tie |
| beg¹ for one's life | be scared | promise |
| **solution** | | |
| send a letter | demand | set free unharmed |
| agree | EXCHANGE HOSTAGES | warn |
| outside the city walls | on Sunday at dawn | give the gold back |

¹to beg [beg] – *bitten*

## 5 Writing: Tips for young apprentices

Your class is preparing a gallery walk with tips on what young apprentices can do in difficult or embarrassing situations. *Advise young apprentices what to do in the following situations. Write three sentences or more for each situation.*

1. Someone you work with makes comments you do not like about your looks, your religion and your family background.

2. A colleague of the opposite sex starts to show interest in you. He/She makes sexist jokes and shows no respect for your personal space.

## 6 Speaking: Being a journalist

Every day we can watch and listen to news reports from political 'hot spots' about armed conflicts, terrorist attacks or natural disasters.
*What motivation, strengths (Stärken) and talents do journalists need who do these reports?*
*What do you think? Would you like to be a journalist? Say why/why not.*
*Make notes first.*

**Notes**

## 7 Mediation: Hong Kong – a former[1] British colony

On June 30, 1997 Hong Kong was given back to China after more than 150 years of being a British colony.

In 1984 Britain and the People's Republic of China drew up a treaty about when and how Hong Kong should be returned to its motherland.
5 Socialist China demanded military control over the region, but declared that it would let Hong Kong keep its democratic system and capitalist market economy for 50 years. There would be "one nation, two systems".

*The flag of Hong Kong till 1997*

Since the 1960s Hong Kong has been one of the leading trading[2] economies in the world and has earned more per head than Britain. The
10 secret of its success is its closeness to China and strong links with the West. Although China is Hong Kong's most important trading partner, the low taxes and the English Common Law system have attracted investors from all over the world for a long time.

In the 1990s Hong Kong developed into a leading financial centre and became one of the richest
15 places in the world. Fortunately[3], giving Hong Kong back to socialist China in 1997 did not stop that development. However, China's change in policy after 2003 has led the people of Hong Kong to call their political system a 'birdcage democracy'. They hope that pressure from the international community will eventually force China to approve of an independent Hong Kong one day.

[1]former ['fɔːmə] – *ehemalig*, [2]trading ['treɪdɪŋ] – *Handels-*, [3]fortunately ['fɔːtʃnətli] – *glücklicherweise*

# EK 2 | Mediation

a) *Bearbeite die Aufgaben.*

1. *In welcher Bedeutung wird folgender Begriff verwendet? Markiere die richtige Bedeutung.*

| **economy** [ɪˈkɒnəmi] *Substantiv* (line 7) | |
|---|---|
| **1.** Sparsamkeit, Wirtschaftlichkeit; | ☐ |
| **2.** a) Sparmaßnahme, b) Einsparung, c) Ersparnis; | ☐ |
| **3.** *Wirtschaft* Wirtschaft (-ssystem *oder* -lehre) | ☐ |

2. *Erschließe die Wortart von „closeness" (l. 10) und die deutsche Bedeutung des Begriffs.*

___

3. *Übertrage „birdcage democracy" (l. 17) in gutes Deutsch.*

___

b) *Finde die Informationen im Text und übertrage sie ins Deutsche.*

1. der politische Status von Hong Kong einst und jetzt:

___

2. die Forderungen und Zugeständnisse Chinas bei der Vertragsaushandlung:

___

3. Hong Kongs wirtschaftlicher Erfolg und die Gründe dafür:

___

4. die Einstellung der Menschen in Hong Kong zu ihrer Regierung:

___

## Topic 3  Our world in our hands

### 1 Listening: A classroom discussion

a) Tick (✔) the right person.

| Who ... | Veejay | Neil | Teacher |
|---|---|---|---|
| 1. leads the discussion? | | | |
| 2. sees a link between $CO_2$ and global warming? | | | |
| 3. has a different opinion? | | | |
| 4. interrupts and should wait? | | | |
| 5. tells someone to let the other finish? | | | |
| 6. warns that global warming will affect animals, plants and people? | | | |
| 7. thinks that we have to act quickly to reduce $CO_2$ emissions? | | | |

b) What does Joanne say? Tick (✔) the <u>four</u> correct boxes.

Joanne says that ...
1. some scientists have clearly shown that the world is not getting warmer.
2. scientists do not agree with her dad.
3. scientists do not agree about the reasons why there is global warming.
4. some scientists believe that not $CO_2$ but other emissions cause global warming.
5. some scientists argue that it is normal that the temperature of the Earth changes.
6. some scientists argue that the world would be getting colder if there was no $CO_2$ emission.
7. she would like the weather to get much warmer.

c) Complete the sentences with the missing words.

**Gillian** says that those scientists who do not believe in global warming are probably paid by

(1) _____ companies. She explains that if all of the

(2) _____ people in Britain just saved (3) _____ ton of

$CO_2$ a year, that there would be (4) _____ tons of $CO_2$ less.

Finally she explains that to save $CO_2$ you can turn the (5) _____ down, wear an extra

(6) _____ and turn off the lights and (7) _____.

**Mark** argues that it is the companies which use most (8) _____.

d) What quality does the discussion have? Tick (✔) the best box.

The statements of the pupils are ...
1. all exactly the same.
2. based on research that the students have done, not just on their opinions.
3. all supporting Joanne's opinion.

## 2 Reading: 'Green' holidays

Many people want to reduce their carbon footprint. In normal everyday life it's quite easy. There are lots of articles about it everywhere. You can leave the car at home and walk or catch the bus. You can buy smaller, more eco-friendly cars. You can turn the TV off – remember not to leave it on standby. You can turn the lights off and the heating down. And you can buy local products. Easy!

5 But what about your holidays? Most people forget about the environment when they go on holiday. They think that it doesn't matter if they waste some energy and some water once a year. It's only for a week or two. It doesn't matter if they fly on a very environmentally unfriendly plane to a hot country. But does it matter? Yes, of course, it does. Every year millions of people fly to places on holiday and to foreign cities for weekend breaks, too. This can increase their carbon footprints by large amounts.

10 So what can you do if you want to have a 'green' holiday? First you have to think about where you want to go. Do you really have to go to that island on the other side of the world? Or could you enjoy a holiday nearer at home? There are lots of advantages[1]. OK it can rain but do you really want to go a country where it is too hot to move (and sometimes too hot to sleep)? If you don't have to travel too far, you won't be tired when you get there. You can get to know[2] your own country and make friends
15 who live nearer home.

Secondly you need to think about how you want to travel. Planes are often quick and cheap but just think of all those $CO_2$ emissions. Planes produce more carbon dioxide than trains or small cars. Why don't you try the train? Trains may take longer, but you can see more out of the window. It's easier to talk to people, read books or play games. When you go by train, it is part of the holiday. Remember
20 your holiday can start when you leave your door and not when you arrive at your hotel in a foreign country. Or why don't you try a bike holiday? That's the best way to see a country and the best way to meet other people. And you don't have to take all your luggage with you on your bike, you can go on an organized holiday and a company will take your luggage for you. Or how about a trip on a boat? That's interesting, fun and something different which you can talk about for years.

25 The last thing to think about is where you are going to stay. In many tourist areas there are big hotels which use lots of energy and lots of water. Why don't you try a 'green' hotel? You can find them all over the world in the most beautiful places. They often have solar energy and their own fruit and vegetable gardens. In smaller places tourists are still guests and not just customers.

[1]advantage [əd'vɑːntɪdʒ] – *Vorteil*, [2]to get to know [ɡet tə 'nəʊ] – *kennen lernen*

a) *Answer the questions. Write notes.*

1. What simple things can people do to reduce their carbon footprint?

_____
_____
_____
_____
_____

2. How much do most people think of the environment when they go on holiday?

_____
_____
_____
_____
_____

Orange Line 6
ISBN 978-3-12-547564-9

© Ernst Klett Verlag GmbH, Stuttgart 2010 | www.klett.de
Von dieser Druckvorlage ist die Vervielfältigung für den eigenen Unterrichtsgebrauch gestattet. Die Kopiergebühren sind abgegolten. Alle Rechte vorbehalten.

3. How far do most people think of the environment when they go on holiday?

_____
_____
_____
_____

b) *Complete the diagram with the facts from the text.*

### environmentally-unfriendly holidays

| places | transport | accomodation¹ |
|---|---|---|
| _____ | _____ | _____ |
| _____ | _____ | _____ |
| _____ | _____ | _____ |

### green holiday alternatives

| places | transport | accomodation |
|---|---|---|
| _____ | _____ | _____ |
| _____ | _____ | _____ |
| _____ | _____ | _____ |

| advantages | advantages | advantages |
|---|---|---|
| _____ | _____ | _____ |
| _____ | _____ | _____ |
| _____ | _____ | _____ |
| _____ | _____ | _____ |
| _____ | _____ | _____ |

¹accommodation [əˌkɒməˈdeɪʃn] – *Unterkunft*

c) *What sort of text is it? Tick (✔) the best box.*

The text is …
1. written by a scientist and explains how people cause pollution when they go on holiday to foreign countries. ☐
2. like an advert which is taken from a website that informs us about 'green' hotels and holidays in the UK. ☐
3. shows that people cause pollution when they go on holiday to foreign countries and gives information about green holiday alternatives. ☐

## 3 Writing: Working with statistics

*Study the diagram. What is the most surprising information given? What advice would you give people?*

| CO₂ emissions for a journey of 150 miles | |
|---|---|
| small car | 28,0 kg |
| large car | 50,0 kg |
| train | 14,5 kg |
| coach | 21,5 kg |
| plane | 38,1 kg |

kg of $CO_2$ per traveller

---

## 4 Writing: Applying for an apprenticeship with *Mc Ltd. Eco Friendly Builders*

You are interested in a career in eco building and are thinking of applying for the following apprenticeship in Scotland.

> ### A career in eco building?
> **Mc Ltd. Eco Friendly Builders** is offering apprenticeships in eco building! The apprenticeships will be in Scotland. Apprentices will get £12,500 per year, plus extra money for training, travel and equipment. You don't need any specific[1] qualifications to apply: all we ask is that you show a lot of interest in your apprenticeship and a strong environmental motivation.
>
> **Post:** Trainee[2] Eco Plumber and Installer
> **Location:** Edinburgh and locations throughout Scotland
> **Duration[3]:** 18 months
> **Start date:** next July
>
> The apprentice will develop skills in planning, installing and repairing piping[4] and heating systems. There will be courses and workshops about eco technologies. The apprentice will work with experts in their field and will find out about and be given experience in practical eco building.
>
> To apply, send the application form and CV/personal profile to: mcltd@live.co.uk

[1]specific [spe'sɪfɪk] – *speziell*, [2]trainee [treɪn'iː] – *in der Ausbildung*, [3]duration [djʊ'reɪʃn] – *Dauer*, [4]piping ['paɪpɪŋ] – *Rohrleitungs-*

a) *Complete the application form.*

---

Mc Ltd. Eco Friendly Builders
130 St. Stephen Street
Edinburgh
EH3 5AD

E-mail: mcltd@live.co.uk

## Mc Ltd.
## Eco Friendly Builders

### *Application Form*

Apprenticeship applied for: _____

**Personal statement:**
(Please tell us about your environmental interests and why you think the apprenticeship will suit you.)

_____
_____
_____
_____
_____
_____
_____
_____
_____
_____
_____
_____

**Personal details:**

Full name: _____  Date of birth: _____

Address: _____

E-mail: _____  Telephone: _____

Is there anything special we should consider?
(Bitte um ein Telefoninterview, weil du in Deutschland wohnst.)

_____
_____

---

b) *Add your CV and/or your personal profile. Use an extra piece of paper.*

## 5 Speaking: A telephone interview with Mrs Burden from *Mc Ltd. Eco Friendly Builders*

Situation: Your family is moving to Edinburgh in Scotland at the end of June because of your father's new job there. You have applied for an apprenticeship with *Mc Ltd. Eco Friendly Builders*. They want to do a telephone interview with you.
*Complete the talk.*

Torsten Begau: _____ *Answer the phone.*

Mrs Burden: This is Eileen Burden from Mc Ltd. Eco Friendly Builders, Edinburgh. Am I speaking to Mr Torsten Begau?

Torsten Begau: _____ *Say yes and say something nice.*

Mrs Burden: Hello, Mr Begau. I'd like to ask you some questions. We don't often get applications from Germany. Why would you like to work in Scotland?

Torsten Begau: _____ *Tell her that your family is moving to Scotland.*

Mrs Burden: I see. And when are you moving to Scotland?

Torsten Begau: _____ *Tell her when you are moving.*

Mrs Burden: Well, that that might be a bit late. You know that the apprenticeship starts on 1st July, don't you?

Torsten Begau: _____ *Say yes. Tell her that you will be finishing school in June and that your family can't leave Germany earlier.*

Mrs Burden: I see. By the way, your English is really good. Is it one of your favourite subjects? What other subjects are you good at?

Torsten Begau: _____ *Say yes and tell her about the subjects you are good at and why you like them.*

Mrs Burden: You wrote about a water project in your personal profile. Could you please explain what you did.

Torsten Begau: _____ *Tell her when and for how long you did the project. Tell her what you did, e.g. checking the quality of the tap water/water in rivers, etc.*

Mrs Burden: I see. There's one last thing I'd like to talk about with you. You know that a plumber's job involves doing dirty and hard work, don't you?

Torsten Begau: _____   *Tell her that you know that and tell her about your strengths (Stärken) and why the job may be the right one for you.*

Mrs Burden: Great. Thanks for the interview, Mr Begau. You'll be hearing from us again soon.

Torsten Begau: _____   *Say something nice and thank her for the call.*

## 6 Mediation: Recycling

*Lies den Text und beantworte die Fragen.*

### Three Tips for 'Greening' Your Water

| | | |
|---|---|---|
| **Get Out Your Wrench:** | Did you know that a dripping faucet can waste 20 gallons (about 75 litres) of water a day and a leaking[1] toilet can use 90,000 gallons (about 320,000 litres) of water in a month? Here's an easy way to use your DO IT YOURSELF skills: repair all the faucets, etc. in your home. | 5 |
| **Roll Out the Barrel:** | By installing some rain barrels, you can collect rainwater for uses like watering[2] your plants or garden. You will need less tap water and will save money and energy.<br><br>You even have plumbing skills? Great! Then install a rain water tank and fix it to your toilet. | 10 |
| **Say No to Bottles:** | Americans buy 30 billion water bottles every year with 845 bottles ending up[3] in landfills[4] every second.<br>These water bottles are made from oil, which is often transported by ship. Just imagine, a water bottle 1/4 full with oil is needed to produce one bottle.<br>Did You Know?<br>• The amount of water per person used by the average American every day is 400 gallons.<br>• The amount of money spent on bottled water in the industrial countries in the world is $35 billion[5]. | 15<br><br>20<br><br>25 |

[1] to leak [liːk] – *lecken*, [2] to water [ˈwɔːtə] – *gießen*, [3] to end up [endˈʌp] – *enden*,
[4] landfill [ˈlændfɪl] – *Mülldeponie*, [5] billion [ˈbɪljən] – *Milliarde*

## Mediation

1. Was soll „grünes Wasser" sein?

2. Wie kann man mit einem Schraubenschlüssel Wasser sparen?

3. Was hat das Fass mit der Gießkanne zu tun?

4. Wieso soll man Nein sagen zu Flaschen? Man soll doch Wasser trinken.

# Topic 3  Our world in our hands

## 1 Listening: A debate

a) *Listen. What's the motion of the debate? Complete the sentence.*

"To save the world each of us has to _____ his or her _____

_____."

b) *Tick (✔) the right person.*

| Who ... | Veejay | Mark | Chairwoman |
|---|---|---|---|
| 1. mentions the motion? | | | |
| 2. sees a direct connection between $CO_2$ emissions and global warming? | | | |
| 3. disagrees with that statement? | | | |
| 4. speaks out of turn and should wait for his turn? | | | |
| 5. tells someone to follow the rules? | | | |
| 6. warns of the impact global warming may have on animals, plants and people? | | | |
| 7. thinks that we must reduce $CO_2$ emissions quickly? | | | |

c) *What arguments does Joanne mention? Tick (✔) the four correct boxes.*

Joanne, a speaker against the motion, argues that ...
1. some scientists have clearly proved that the world is not getting warmer.
2. scientists disagree about global warming.
3. scientists disagree about the reasons why we are facing global warming.
4. some scientists believe that not $CO_2$ but other toxic emissions are responsible for global warming.
5. some scientists argue that it is normal that the temperature of the Earth changes.
6. some scientists think that we will be facing the next ice age soon.

d) *Complete the sentences with the missing words or numbers.*

**Gillian** says that those scientists who do not accept that there is a connection between $CO_2$

emissions and global warming are probably paid by (1) _____.

She explains that if all of the (2) _____ people who live in Britain just

saved (3) _____ ton of $CO_2$ per year, that that would mean

(4) _____ tons of $CO_2$ less. Finally she says that if everybody made a

(5) _____ difference on their own, then all the people on the Earth could

make a (6) _____ difference (7) _____.

**Mark** argues that in his opinion people are on this Earth to (8) _____ and not to worry about everything. He blames the (9) _____ and says that they must reduce their (10) _____.

e) *What quality does the debate have? Tick (✔) the best box.*

The arguments of the speakers are …
1. all exactly the same.
2. based on research that the students have done, not just on their opinions.
3. all supporting the motion.

## 2 Reading: 'Green' holidays

Many people want to reduce their carbon footprint. In normal everyday life it's quite easy. There are lots of articles about it everywhere. You can leave the car at home and walk or catch the bus. You can buy smaller, more eco-friendly cars. You can turn the TV off and not leave it on standby. You can make sure you turn the lights off and the heating down. And you can buy local products. Easy!

5 But what about when it comes to holidays? Most people feel that they only go on holiday once a year and it doesn't matter if they waste a little more than usual. It's only a week or two out of 52. It doesn't matter if they fly on a very environmentally unfriendly plane to a hot country and use water the people there haven't got enough of to wash their towels[1] every day and fill their swimming pools. But does it matter? Yes, of course, it does. Every year millions of people fly to places they don't need
10 to visit and increase their carbon footprints by large amounts. In these days of cheap flights people also fly to foreign cities for a weekend break and never think about how they are damaging our environment. So what can you do if you want to have a green holiday? Well, there are lots of ways if you are prepared to try something different. First you have to think about where you want to go. Do you really have to go to that island on the other side of the world? Or could you enjoy staying nearer
15 home? In the east of Great Britain it does not rain very often and the south of England is warm. Do you really need to go somewhere where it is too hot to move (and sometimes too hot to sleep)? There are lots of advantages to staying nearer home. If you don't have to travel too far, you will be more relaxed when you arrive. You can get to know your own country and make friends who live nearer home.

20 Secondly you need to think about how you are going to travel. Planes are often quick and cheap but just think of all that carbon dioxide which they produce. Planes have the highest emissions of carbon dioxide per person of all methods[2] of travel. Why don't you try the train? Trains may take longer, but you can relax on a train, read a book, play games, talk to people or just look out of the window. When you go by train, it is part of the holiday.

25 Remember your holiday can start when you leave your door not when you arrive at your hotel in a foreign country. Travelling by train is also a lot healthier than travelling by plane or by car. Or why don't you try going on a cycling holiday? Cycling is the best way to see a country and the best way to meet other people. And you don't have to take all your luggage with you on your bike: you can go on an organised holiday where your luggage is transported for you from one hotel or bed and breakfast
30 to another. Great Britain is great for cycling with its miles of coasts and beautiful countryside[3]. Why don't you try cycling around Cornwall or from the east coast of Britain to the west? You know you'll feel good when you arrive. Or how about a trip on a canal boat? It's interesting, relaxing, fun and something different which you can talk about for years.

The last thing to think about is where you are going to stay. In many tourist areas there are big hotels
35 which use lots of energy and lots of water when the people who live locally don't have enough. Is that necessary? No! Why don't you try a green hotel or bed and breakfast place? You can find them all over the world in the most beautiful places.

They often have solar energy and some even grow their own food. But it doesn't matter which place you choose, you know that you will meet people who think like you and you will have a holiday which is a little different from the holidays you have had before.

[1]towel ['taʊəl] – *Handtuch*, [2]method ['meθəd] – *Methode*, [3]countryside ['kʌntrisaɪd] – *Landschaft*

a) *Answer the questions. Write notes.*

**1.**
- What is the text about?
- What does the author try to convince the readers of?

**2.**
- What does the author write about in the introduction?

**3.**
- What does the author criticise first?
- What examples does the author give to prove his/her view?
- What alternative does the author suggest?
- What advantages does the author see with this alternative?

— author criticises first the fact that most people feel that they can forget about the environment for a week or two on holiday

**4.**
- What does the author criticise next?
- What alternatives does the author suggest?
- What advantages does the author see in this alternative?
- What other alternatives does the author suggest?
- What advantages does the author see with those alternatives?

**5.**
- What does the author criticise finally?
- What alternatives does the author suggest?
- What advantages does the author see with those alternatives?

b) *What sort of text is it? Tick (✔) the best box.*

The text is …
1. scientific and explains the impact of people's holidays on the environment in detail. ☐
2. like an advert about 'green' hotels and holidays and adventures in the UK. ☐
3. written in a popular style and shows that most people's holiday is environmentally unfriendly and suggests eco-friendlier ways of spending one's holidays. ☐

## 3 Writing: Working with statistics

a) *Analyse the table. Think of the absolute amount, the amount per person and which countries have the worst and the least pollution from airplanes. Start like this:*

**$CO_2$ emissions from planes in the EU (2009)**

| Country | $CO_2$ (million tons) | $CO_2$ per person |
|---|---|---|
| UK | 60.3 | 0.98 |
| Germany | 41.9 | 0.51 |
| France | 30.9 | 0.48 |
| Spain | 27.1 | 0.59 |
| Italy | 17.7 | 0.29 |
| Netherlands | 17.1 | 1.07 |
| Total EU | 235.7 | |

*The UK has the highest amount of $CO_2$ emissions from planes in the EU*

b) *Study the graph: What is the most surprising information given? What do you suggest that people should do?*

| | CO₂ emissions for a journey of 150 miles |
|---|---|
| small car | 28,0 kg |
| large car | 50,0 kg |
| train | 14,5 kg |
| coach | 21,5 kg |
| plane | 38,1 kg |

kg of CO₂ per traveller

## 4 Writing: Applying for an apprenticeship with *Natural Talent*

You are interested in a career in the environmental sector and are thinking of applying for the following apprenticeship in Scotland.

### A career in the environmental sector?

**Natural Talent** is training the next generation of naturalists[1]! The apprenticeships will be based in Scotland, receive a bursary[2] of £12,500 per year, plus extra money for training, travel and equipment. You don't need any formal qualifications to apply: all we ask is that you show a lot of interest in your chosen apprenticeship and a strong environmental motivation.

**Post:** BTCV Natural Talent Apprentice[3] Grassland Ecologist[4]
**Location:** Royal Botanic Garden Edinburgh and locations all over Scotland
**Duration:** 18 months
**Start date:** July of the following year

The apprentice will learn how to identify, survey and monitor wild flowers and their habitats[5]. There will be field courses and workshops. The apprentice will work with experts in the field and will gain knowledge and experience in practical grassland conservation[6].

To apply send the application form and CV/personal profile to: Natural-Talent@btcv.org.uk

[1]naturalist ['nætʃrlɪst] – *Naturforscher/in*, [2]bursary ['bɜːsri] – *hier: Stipendium*, [3]apprentice [əˈprentɪs] – *Lehrling*, [4]ecologist [ɪˈkɒlədʒɪst] – *Ökologe/Ökologin*, [5]habitat [ˈhæbɪtæt] – *Lebensraum*, [6]conservation [ˌkɒnsəˈveɪʃn] — *Schutz/Erhaltung*

a) *Complete the application form.*

Natural Talent BTCV Scotland
Balallan House
24 Allan Park
Stirling
FK8 2QG

**E-mail:** Natural-Talent@btcv.org.uk

# natural talent

## Application Form

Apprenticeship applied for: _____

**Personal statement:**
*(Please tell us about your environmental interests and why you think the apprenticeship will suit you.)*

_____
_____
_____
_____
_____
_____
_____
_____
_____
_____

**Personal details:**

Full name: _____  Date of birth: _____

Address: _____

E-mail: _____  Telephone: _____

Is there anything special we should consider?
*(Bitte um ein Telefoninterview, weil du in Deutschland wohnst.)*

_____
_____

b) *Add your CV and/or your personal profile. Use an extra sheet of paper.*

# 5 Speaking: A telephone interview with Mrs Burden from *Natural Talent*

Situation: You have applied for an apprenticeship with *Natural Talent*. They have offered you the opportunity of a telephone interview.
*Complete the talk.*

Susann Begau: _____   *Melde dich.*

Mrs Burden: This is Eileen Burden from Natural Talent, Edinburgh. Am I speaking to Ms Susann Begau?

Susann Begau: _____   *Bejahe und sage etwas Nettes.*

Mrs Burden: Hello, Ms Begau. I'd like to ask you some questions. You see, we don't often get applications from Germany. Why would you like to work in Scotland?

Susann Begau: _____   *Erkläre, dass deine Mutter Biologin ist und schon in einer Wasseraufbereitungsanlage in Edinburgh gearbeitet hat. Daher kennst du das Land und würdest dort auch gern arbeiten.*

Mrs Burden: I see. And when could you come here?

Susann Begau: _____   *Sage, dass du Ende Juni kommen könntest.*

Mrs Burden: Well, I'm afraid that that might be a bit late. You know that the apprenticeship starts on July 1, do you?

Susann Begau: _____   *Bejahe. Sage, dass du Mitte Juni die Schule abschließt und deine Familie dann noch umzieht.*

Mrs Burden: I see. By the way, your English is quite good. Is it one of your favourite subjects and what other subjects are you good at?

Susann Begau: _____   *Bejahe und sage, dass auch Biologie und andere Naturwissenschaften deine Lieblingsfächer sind und warum.*

| | | |
|---|---|---|
| Mrs Burden: | You mentioned a water project in your personal profile. Could you please explain what you did. | |
| Susann Begau: | _____ _____ _____ _____ _____ | *Sage, dass ihr eine Woche lang euch beschäftigt habt mit der Qualität des Leitungswassers und wie rein bzw. giftig das Wasser in Flüssen und Teichen ist.* |
| Mrs Burden: | I see. There's one last thing I'd like to talk about with you. You know that you'll be working outside most of the time and that it can be quite cold and windy in Scotland. | |
| Susann Begau: | _____ _____ _____ _____ | *Sage, dass du dir dessen bewusst bist und dass du gern in der freien Natur bist.* |
| Mrs Burden: | Great. Thanks for the interview, Ms Begau. You'll hear again from us soon. | |
| Susann Begau: | _____ _____ _____ | *Sage etwas Nettes und bedanke dich für den Anruf.* |

## 6 Mediation: Recycling

Situation: Du hast folgende E-Mail von deinem englischen Freund erhalten. Er ist nicht so gut in Deutsch, deshalb hilf ihm und gib ihm die notwendigen Erklärungen. Du informierst dich vorsichtshalber noch einmal. Beziehe dich auf den Text über das Duale System.

| From: | steve@xyz.com |
|---|---|
| To: | friend@xyz.de |
| Re: | Help! |

Hi there,
this is just a short call for help. I wonder if you'd help me with my project on recycling systems in Europe. Please explain to me what you Germans do with the "Gelber Sack" and what "Grüner Punkt" means. Of course I know that they're "yellow bag" and "green dot" in English, but what's behind them? I thought that you had bottle and paper banks where you could take your glass and paper waste. Did they stop them in Germany?
Thanks a lot.
Steve

Die **Duales System Deutschland GmbH** ist ein privates Unternehmen, das die Sammlung und Sortierung von Verkaufsverpackungen betreibt. Über dieses Unternehmen entsorgbare Verpackungen sind mit dem Grünen Punkt gekennzeichnet.

Im Gelben Sack werden ausschließlich Verkaufsverpackungen aus Kunststoff, Metall oder Verbundmaterialien entsorgt, die mit dem grünen Punkt versehen sind. Manche Bundesländer haben anstatt des Gelben Sacks die Gelbe Tonne eingeführt.

Gebrauchsgegenstände aus den o.g. Materialien wie z.B. Videokassetten, CDs oder DVDs gehören nicht in den Gelben Sack.

Behälter aus Glas sind weiterhin im Altglascontainer zu entsorgen und Verpackungen aus Pappe oder Papier gehören zum Altpapier oder in den Papiercontainer.

Beispiele für Verpackungen, die über den Gelben Sack bzw. die Gelbe Tonne entsorgt werden:
- Verpackungen aus Kunststoff : Behälter für Körperpflegemittel, Joghurtbecher etc.
- Verpackungen aus Metall: Getränke- und Konservendosen, Metallverschlüsse etc.
- Verpackungen aus Verbundstoffen: Milch-, Saft- und Weinkartons

---

From: friend@xyz.de
To: steve@xyz.com
Re: Help!

Hi Steve,

## Topic 4  Choices and decisions

### 1 Listening: Sex at 16?

a) *What are David's ideas about his holiday? Tick (✔) the correct boxes.*

1. He wants to spend his holiday here.

Sophia

Dartmoor

2. He wants to stay in a …

3. He wants to spend his holiday with …

his mum and dad ☐   Sophie ☐
Sophie, his mum and dad ☐   Sophie and her mum ☐

b) *How does David's mum feel about David's holiday plans? Complete the sentence with a few words only.*

David's mum _____

_____.

c) *What embarrassing questions does David's mum ask? Tick (✔) the <u>four</u> correct boxes.*

David's mum asks …
1. if Sophie's mum knows about the holiday.
2. if David knows how old he is.
3. where David has found out about the legal age.
4. if David has learnt how to make sure that he won't become a father.
5. if David's girlfriend has already had sex.
6. if David has already had sex.
7. if David has talked to his father about the question of sex.
8. what his father's opinion is about sex at 16.

d) *What advice does David's mum give? Complete the sentences with the missing words.*

As Sophie's partner David needs to make sure that they're both (1) _____ as long as they haven't finished their education. It takes two people to have a baby and both partners are (2) _____ .

e) *Which heading goes best with the talk between David and his mum?*
*Tick (✔).*

1. I'm not a baby any more!
2. It's never easy for a mum to see her child has grown up.
3. It's hard to understand these teenagers of today.

## 2 Reading: Salford College

**Are you leaving school?**
We offer a range of courses at different levels to prepare you for your career. Our courses build on each other so you can choose the right level for you and continue until you get the qualification which you need to get a job.

**What do you need to do?**
First you need to choose which career you would like to go into and then choose the right level for you. When you have decided on the course you would like, you need to apply for it.

**How do you apply?**
First you need to fill in our application form. You can get this from the college or download it from our website. You need to send it to us before the 30th April. If you have any questions about the form or need help to fill it in, you can contact our office. When we have received your application, we will invite you for an interview.

**Choose a course**
Before you choose your course, you need to decide on your career. It is often a good idea to try different internships and to talk to people who work in that career. If you are not sure, you can choose an introductory course to find out whether it is the right subject for you.

**Business Studies**

In this course you learn about the different areas in the real world of business. There are courses in human resources, marketing, sales, finance and public relations. Students learn to develop the skills which they will need for their career in business.

You can choose from two courses:

| | |
|---|---|
| **Level 1:** | Students should be interested in business and be good at Maths and English. You will develop basic skills in business. Qualifications in IT can be done at the same time. Your study plan may include work experience or a placement within a specific field of employment. After completing this course you may find employment within sales, customer services or reception work, though limited. We usually advise our students to start the level 2 course. |
| **Level 2 (Diploma in Business):** | Students should have 4 GCSEs with at least grade D. During this course you will need to work for two weeks in a business of your choice. After the course you can start your career in the world of business or go on to do the Advanced Diploma in Business. |

# GK 4 — Reading

a) *Complete the flow chart to show the steps you must take when you plan your education at Salford College.*

```
          You are sure about your career and the course you want to choose.
                    │                                         │
                   YES                                        NO
                    │                                         │
          Before you apply:  ◄──────────────────────  What you can do:
```

- _____          • _____

- _____          • _____

- _____          • _____

         │
  How you   • _____
  apply:    ( _____ )
            _____
         │
  When you have applied: _____

b) *Complete the following with the right words from the text.*

| How do you know that you will learn how to … | There is a course in … |
|---|---|
| 1. manage all the employees in a company/organisation? | _____ |
| 2. spend and save money successfully? | _____ |
| 3. work with the media and how to make things public? | _____ |
| 4. sell products or services? | _____ |
| 5. plan advertising actions for products or services? | _____ |

c) *Compare the two levels Salford offers by completing the table below.*

|  | level 1 | level 2 |
|---|---|---|
| Which qualities/ school qualifications should you have? |  |  |
| What qualification will you get? |  |  |
| Will the qualification be enough to start a job? (yes/no/not certain) |  |  |
| What kinds of further qualification are there after finishing it? |  |  |

## 3 Writing: Giving further information

*Answer Mr Grand's e-mail and his questions. Start with "Dear Mr Grand ..."*

| From: | william.grand@salford-col.ac.uk | Quick Address List |
|---|---|---|
| To: |  |  |

Dear ...,
Thank you for your application to Salford College. We have received your application for Business Studies and are contacting you for further information on your school leaving examinations and in support of your application.
To find you the right course level please explain what final exams you will be taking, what skills are tested in the different exams and the grades you hope to get.
Please, tell us also about any volunteer work, internships and summer jobs you have done or any work experience you have.
I look forward to hearing from you.
Yours sincerely
William Grand
------------------------------------------------
Study Support Administrative Assistant
Salford City College

_____

_____

_____

_____

## 4 Writing: Giving advice

*Choose one of the following letters and answer it. What would you advise the person to do?*

| | |
|---|---|
| **(1)** Dear Agony Angel,<br>I'm a 15 year old boy and in Year 11 at school. I'm taking my GCSEs next year. I can't sleep at night worrying about my grades and exams, and I don't go out anymore because I don't have the time. I am at breaking point! Please help me! Yours, Robert | |
| **(2)** Hi there,<br>I'm afraid my friend has a drinking problem and I'm fed up with always hanging around in pubs and ending up drunk. Every time he drinks I start to drink, too, because everything is much easier when I'm a little drunk myself. I don't know what to do. Molly (16) | |

| **(3)** Dear Christopher,<br>I have a very personal problem: I've missed my period for 2 months and a half and may be expecting a baby. I'm sixteen years old and I go to comprehensive school. My parents will kill me. What should I do?! Please help me! Love, Cathy | **(4)** Dear Agony Angel Christopher,<br>I'm fed up with my mum and dad. I've got a disabled[1] brother and my parents give him all their love. If my brother does anything wrong, they never seem to say very much but if I do anything wrong, I always get into trouble. Sometimes I feel really angry. Ben (14) |
|---|---|

[1]disabled [dɪˈseɪbld] – *behindert*

Speaking/Writing  4 GK

## 5 Speaking/Writing: In a chat room

Situation: Sam has invited you to her private chat room. Your nick is Baba.
*Complete the chat. Look at the following chat words:*

| WC = welcome | thx = thanks | u = you | r = are | 2 = too/to | IC = I see | TNT = till next time |

Sam: WC to my chat room, Baba!

Baba: _Thx_ _____  *Say hello to your chat partner and ask her for her age and where she lives.*

Sam: I'm 16. I'm from a small place near Liverpool. And u?

Baba: _____  *Answer and ask her if she is still at school.*

Sam: Yes, but I'm in my final year and will be leaving soon. R u still at school, 2?

Baba: _____  *Answer and tell her when you will finish school and what final exams you will take.*

Sam: IC. I've already taken 4 GCSEs, but I still have to sit English, Maths and Science in June.

Baba: _____  *Ask her if she has already decided what she wants to do after school.*

Sam: Well, if I get grades A–C in Maths and Science, I can start an apprenticeship as a technician at Vauxhall Motors.

Baba: _____  *Tell her that her plans to start an apprenticeship at Vauxhall Motors sound interesting and ask her if she has any work experience fixing cars.*

Sam: Sure. I've helped out at my uncle's garage lots of times. Why? Do u have a flat tyre? ;-)

Baba: _____  *Tell her you don't need help with a car. Ask her where she wants to work later on.*

Sam: Well, a job with a big company would be great – and later on my own car repair shop. And u?

Baba: _____  *Tell her what career you are thinking of and what hopes and dreams you have.*

Sam: Sounds cool! Good luck 2 u! Bye. TNT

Baba: _____  *Say something nice and say goodbye.*

## 6 Mediation: The Amish ['ɑːmɪʃ] people

**Where did the Amish come from?**
In the 17th century some people in Europe decided to break away from the traditional church and form their own religious sect. They called themselves "Amish" after their leader Amman. In the 18th century the Amish moved to America. Today there are about 231,000 Amish living in 28 US states.

**What do the Amish believe?**
The Amish believe in God and Jesus.

They stay away from the rest of the world. To show that they are different, they wear clothes that look like the clothes people wore 200 years ago; they speak a different language and do not use any technology or electricity (no cars, radios, telephones, computers or TVs).

**What do Amish teens do?**
Amish teens are only allowed to go to school for eight years. There are about three to four students in each year. Lessons include reading, writing, spelling, English and Math. Other subjects are Health, Geography and History. Kids can do sports during breaks but do not have any other activities. After finishing school, boys find jobs in factories or agriculture, work on the family farm or in the family business. Unmarried girls may work in nearby homes or in Amish shops. Married women are responsible for their home and children.

### A tough decision

When Amish teens reach 16, they enter Rumspringa, a time when they are free from Amish rules. They are allowed to experience life in the outside world including trendy clothes, telephones, alcohol, sex, drugs and wild parties.

By giving them so much freedom, their parents hope they will learn enough to help them make the most important decision of their lives. The Amish teens must decide if they want to join the Amish church and forever give up all non-Amish activities, or if they want to live out in the world and forever leave their families.

Around age 20, when Rumspringa is over, about 90% return to the Amish community.

*Lies die Informationen und fasse zusammen, …*

1. was du über die Herkunft der Amischen erfährst.

2. was typisch ist für die amische Religion.

3. welche Schulbildung die amischen Kinder erhalten.

4. was „Rumspringa" ist und welche Entscheidung amische Teenager treffen müssen.

## 7 Speaking: A life without electricity

*Look at the photos. Imagine you had to live without electricity: No TV, DVDs, radio, CD-player. The telephone is dead. Forget about the Internet. There are no cars, just buggies[1]. You finished school at 13 and work in the fields or at home. That's the way most Amish teenagers live. Welcome to a life of hard physical work!*
*Would you like to live the simple life of the Amish people? Say why/why not.*

[1]buggy ['bʌgi] – *Kutsche*

**Notes**

## Topic 4  Choices and decisions

### 1 Listening: Sex at 16?

a) *What are David's ideas about his holiday? Tick (✔) the correct boxes.*

1. He wants to spend his holiday here.

Sophia ☐

Dartmoor ☐

2. He wants to stay in a …

 ☐

 ☐

3. He wants to spend his holiday with …

his mum and dad ☐  Sophie ☐
Sophie, his mum and dad ☐  Mike and Eric ☐
Sophie and her mum ☐  Sophie, Mike and Eric ☐

b) *How do David's mum and dad feel about David's holiday plans? Complete the sentences with a few words only.*

David's mum _____.

David's dad _____.

c) *What embarrassing questions does David's mum ask? Tick (✔) the <u>four</u> correct boxes.*

David's mum asks …
1. if David knows how old he is.
2. where David has learnt about the legal age.
3. if David has learnt how to avoid pregnancies.
4. if David knows about the many different ways of how to avoid pregnancies.
5. if David's girlfriend has already had sex.
6. if David has already had sex.
7. if David has talked to his father about the question of sex.
8. what his father's opinion is about sex at 16.

d) *What advice does David's mum give? Complete the sentences with the missing words.*

As Sophie's partner David needs to make sure that they're (1) _____ as long as they

haven't finished their education. Of course, both partners are (2) _____.

Having sex is more than just (3) _____ because you have (4) _____

_____ for your partner. Each partner needs to make sure not

to (5) _____ the other one.

e) *Which heading goes best with the talk between David and his mum? Tick (✔).*

1. I'm not a baby any more!
2. It's never easy for a mum to realise her child has become an adult.
3. It's hard to understand these teenagers of today.

## 2 Reading: Salford College

**Are you leaving school?**
We offer a range of courses at different levels to prepare you for your career. Our courses build on each other so you can choose the right level for you and continue until you get the qualification which you need whether you want to go to university or get a job.

**What do you need to do?**
First you need to choose which career you would like to go into and then choose the right level for you. When you have decided on the course you would like, you need to apply for it.

**How do you apply?**
First you need to fill in our application form. You can get this from the college or download it from our website. You need to send it to us before the 30th April. If you have any questions about the form or need help to fill it in, you can contact our office. When we have received your application, we will invite you for an interview.

**Choose a course**
Before you choose your course, you need to decide on your career. It is often a good idea to try different internships and to talk to people who work in that career. If you are not sure, you can choose an introductory course to find out whether it is the right subject for you. Below is a list of subjects and courses in alphabetical order.

**Animal Care**
**Art and Design**
**Building**
**Business Studies**

In Business Studies you learn about the different areas in the real world of business. There are courses in human resources, marketing, sales, finance and public relations. Students learn to develop the practical and personal skills which they will need for their career in business. During the course students can concentrate on the sector of industry which they are most interested in. You can choose from three courses:

**Level 1:** Students should be interested in business and be good at Maths and English. You will gain basic[1] skills in business. Qualifications in IT can be done at the same time. Your study plan may include work experience or a placement[2] within a special field of employment. After completing this course you may find employment within sales, customer services or reception work, though limited. We usually advise our students to take the course leading to the first diploma.

**Level 2** Students should have 4 GCSEs with at least grade D. There are no
**(Diploma in Business):** exams in the course; you will be marked[3] on coursework. During this course you will need to do a placement in a business of your choice. After the course you can start your career in the world of business or go on to do the Advanced Diploma in Business.

**Level 3** Students should have at least 4 GCSEs with grades A–C. The course
**(Advanced Diploma** will concentrate on finance, communication, IT skills and personal skills
**in Business):** and will include a placement in a business of your choice. After the course you can start your career in the world of business or start a university course.

[1]basic ['beɪsɪk] – *Grund-*, [2](work) placement ['pleɪsmənt] – *Praktikum*, [3]to mark [mɑːk] – *hier: benoten*

a) *Complete the flow chart to show the steps you must take when you plan your education at Salford College.*

```
          You are sure about your career and the course you want to choose.
                    ↓                                        ↓
                  YES                                       NO
                    ↓                                        ↓
          Before you apply:  ←─────────────────  What you can do:
```

- _____                • _____
  _____                  _____

- _____                • _____
  _____                  _____

- _____                • _____
  _____                  _____

                                                • _____

How you apply:    ( _____ )
                  _____

When you have applied:   • _____

b) *Complete the following with the right words from the text.*

| How do you know that you will learn how to … | There is a course in … |
|---|---|

1. manage all the employees in a company/organisation?    _____

2. spend, save and invest money successfully?    _____

3. use what you have learnt in the work live?    _____

4. work with the media and how to make things public?    _____

5. sell products or services?    _____

6. plan advertising campaigns for products or services?    _____

7. use your strengths best and learn how to work on your weaknesses?    _____

c) *Compare the three levels Salford offers by completing the grid.*

|  | level 1 | level 2 | level 3 |
|---|---|---|---|
| Which qualities/ school qualifications should you have? | | | |
| What qualification will you gain? | | | |
| Will you gain practical skills? (yes/no/not certain) | | | |
| Will the qualification be enough to start a job? (yes/no/not certain) | | | |
| What kinds of further qualification are there after finishing it? | | | |

d) *Complete the diagram to show how flexible Salford's course system is. Label the levels from 1 to 4 and use arrows (↑) to make it clear.*

**SALFORD COLLEGE**

**Higher Education** | **Employment**

A-Levels
(GCSEs at grades A–C)

Advanced Courses
(GCSEs at grades A–C)

Intermediate Courses
(GCSEs at grades D)

Basic Courses
(GCSEs at grades E–F)

## 3 Writing: Giving further information

*Reply to Mr Grand's e-mail and answer his questions. Start with "Dear Mr Grand …"*

| From: | william.grand@salford-col.ac.uk | Quick Address List |
|---|---|---|
| To: | | |

Dear …,

Thank you for your application to Salford College. We have received your application for Business Studies and are contacting you for further information on your school leaving exams and in support of your application.

To find the right course level for you, please explain what final exams you will be taking, what skills are tested in the different exams and the grades you hope to get.

Please tell us also about any volunteer work, placements and summer jobs you have done or work experience you have gained.

Thank you for your cooperation and I look forward to hearing from you.

Yours sincerely
William Grand
--------------------------------------------
Study Support Administrative Assistant
Salford City College

## 4 Writing: Giving advice

*Choose two of the following letters and answer them. What would you advise the people to do?*

**(1)** Dear Agony Angel,
I'm a 15-year-old boy and in Year 11 at school. I'm taking my GCSEs next year and I cannot cope with the pressure from my school and my parents. I can't sleep at night because I worry about my grades, and I don't go out any more because I don't have the time. I can't go on! Please help me! Yours, Robert

**(2)** Hi there,
I'm afraid my friend has a drinking problem and I'm fed up with always hanging around in pubs and ending up drunk. Every time he drinks, I feel I have to drink, too, because I can cope so much better when I'm a little drunk myself. I don't know what to do. Molly (16)

**(3)** Dear Christopher,
I have a very personal problem: I'm in 2 months and a half of pregnancy. I'm sixteen years old and I go to comprehensive school. My parents will kill me. What should I do?! I'm desperate, please help me! Love, Cathy

**(4)** Dear Agony Angel Christopher,
I'm fed up with my mum and dad. I've got a disabled[1] brother and he gets more attention than I do. If my brother does anything wrong, they never seem to say very much but if I do anything wrong, I always get into trouble. Sometimes I feel really angry. Ben (14)

[1] disabled [dɪˈseɪbld] – *behindert*

# 5 Speaking/Writing: In a chat room

Situation: Sam has invited you to his/her private chat room. Your nick is Baba.
Complete the chat. Look at the following chat words:

| WC = welcome | thx = thanks | u = you | r = are | 2 = too/to | IC = I see | TNT = till next time |

Sam: WC to my chat room, Baba!

Baba: Thx _____  
_____  
_____  
Begrüße deine/n Chat-Partner/in. Erfrage Alter, Geschlecht u. Wohnort.

Sam: I'm a girl and I'm 16. I'm from a small place near Liverpool. And u?

Baba: _____  
_____  
_____  
Antworte und frage, ob Sam noch zur Schule geht.

Sam: Yes, but I'm in my final year and will be leaving soon. R u still at school, 2?

Baba: _____  
_____  
_____  
_____  
_____  
Antworte und sage, wann du die Schule beendest und welche Prüfungen du in den letzten Schulwochen ablegst.

Sam: IC. I've already taken 4 GCSEs, but I still have to sit English, Maths and Science in June.

Baba: _____  
_____  
_____  
_____  
Frage, ob Sam sich schon entschieden hat, welche Laufbahn sie nach dem Schulabschluss einschlagen will.

Sam: Well, if I get grades A–C in Maths and Science, I can start an apprenticeship as a technician at Vauxhall Motors. It'll be much more than simply on-the job-training. I'll be at the GM training centre, 2.

Baba: _____  
_____  
_____  
_____  
_____  
Du findest es toll, dass Sam eine Ausbildung in der Automobilfertigung machen will. Frage, ob sie schon einmal ein Praktikum in der Autoindustrie gemacht hat.

Sam: I wouldn't do it if I didn't know about it.

Baba: _____ *Entschuldige dich. Frage sie, ob sie später in der Fertigung oder im Kundendienst arbeiten will.*

Sam: I'd like to do both and later have my own car repair shop. And u?

Baba: _____ *Erkläre Sam, welche beruflichen Ziele und Wünsche du hast.*

Sam: Wow! Sounds great! Good luck 2 u! Bye. TNT

Baba: _____ *Sage etwas Nettes zu Sam und verabschiede dich.*

## 6 Mediation: The Amish ['ɑːmɪʃ] people

**A tough decision?**
Whether to wear jeans, own a mobile, go to high school and be shut out of your family's life for the rest of your days? Or to wear long dresses, finish school after the eighth year, live without electricity and stay close to your family and friends?
A tough decision? But these are the alternatives an Amish teenager has got.

**Where did the Amish come from?**
In the 17th century some people in Europe decided to break away from the traditional church and form their own religious sect. They called themselves "Amish" after their leader Amman. In the 18th century the Amish moved to America. Today there are about 231,000 Amish living in 28 US states.

**What do the Amish believe?**
The Amish believe in God and Jesus. They believe that *The Bible* is God's truthful word. The Amish also stay separate from the rest of the world so they can focus on God. To show they are different, they wear traditional clothing; speak a different language and don't use any technology including electricity, cars, radios, telephones, computers and TVs.

### What do Amish teens do?
Amish teens face tight restrictions on their education and are only allowed to go to school for eight years. An Amish school is usually a one-room schoolhouse with no electricity. There are about three to four students in each year. There is one teacher (mostly female) who is Amish and who has no more than eighth grade education herself. Lessons focus on reading, writing, spelling, English and Math. Other subjects are Health, Geography and History. Kids can do sports during breaks but do not have any additional activities. After finishing school, boys find jobs in factories or agriculture, work on the family farm or in the family business. Unmarried girls may work in nearby homes or in Amish shops. Once women marry, they have full responsibility for their home and children.

### How can Amish teens determine which lifestyle fits them?
When Amish teens get 16, they enter Rumspringa, a time when they are set free from Amish rules and restrictions. During that time they are allowed to gain their own experiences in the tempting outside world. For some, to be on their own, and experiment with alcohol, sex, trendy clothes, telephones, drugs and wild parties can be too much to cope with.
By allowing them such freedom, their parents hope they will learn enough to help them make the most important decision of their lives – whether to join the Amish church and forever give up all non-Amish activities, or to stay out in the world, and forever be separated from their families.
Around age 20, when Rumspringa is over, about 90% return to the Amish community.

*Lies die Informationen und fasse zusammen, …*

1. vor welcher Entscheidung amische Teenager stehen.

___

2. was du über die Herkunft der Amischen erfährst.

___

3. was typisch ist für die amische Religion.

___

4. welche Schulbildung die amischen Kinder erhalten.

5. was „Rumspringa" ist und welche Bedeutung es für die Amischen hat.

## 7 Speaking: A life without electricity

*Look at the photos. Imagine you had to live without electricity: no TV, DVDs, radio, CD-player. The telephone is dead. Forget about the Internet. There are no cars, just buggies[1]. You finished school at 13 and work in the fields or at home. That's the way most Amish teenagers live. Welcome to a life of hard physical work!*
*Would you like to live the simple life the Amish people lead? Say why/why not.*

[1]buggy ['bʌgi] – *Kutsche*

# Orange Line 6

## Audio-CD

Hörverstehenstexte zu den Standardaufgaben

| Track | Unit | Übung | Seite | Text/Übungstitel | Spielzeit |
|---|---|---|---|---|---|
| 1 | GK 1 | 1 | 4 | Listening: Interview for a job | 3'32" |
| 2 | GK 2 | 1 | 19 | Listening: Talking about work experience | 3'24" |
| 3 | GK 3 | 1 | 35 | Listening: A classroom discussion | 3'39" |
| 4 | GK 4 | 1 | 52 | Listening: Sex at 16? | 2'43''' |
| 5 | EK 1 | 1 | 11 | Listening: Interview for a job | 4'22" |
| 6 | EK 2 | 1 | 27 | Listening: Talking about work experience | 4'04" |
| 7 | EK 3 | 1 | 43 | Listening: A debate | 4'13" |
| 8 | EK 4 | 1 | 61 | Listening: Sex at 16? | 3'13" |

Gesamtspielzeit: 29'15"

## Lehrersoftware-CD

### Empfohlene Systemvoraussetzungen:

- PC mit 500 MHz oder höher
- Windows 2000, XP, Vista (32 bit), Windows 7
- 128 MB RAM
- S-VGA-kompatible Grafikkarte mit 16,7 Mio Farben (24 bit)
- mind. 50 MB bis max. 200 MB freier Speicherplatz bei Kopie der Medien auf die Festplatte
- 24fach CD-ROM-Laufwerk
- Bildschirmauflösung (Programm) 800 x 600 Pixel
- Schwarzweiß- oder Farbdrucker mit 300 dpi Druckauflösung
- Microsoft Word (ab Version 2000) oder OpenOffice (ab Version 2.0)

Abspiel-Umgebungen und Datei-Betrachter für die Medien befinden sich auf der CD-ROM.

### Schnellstart der Software:

Die Installation kopiert das Programm auf die Festplatte Ihres Rechners. Wir empfehlen, die Medien sofort auf der Festplatte zu installieren. Sie brauchen dann die CD-ROM nicht mehr einzulegen, um das Programm zu verwenden.

- Legen Sie die Lehrersoftware-CD in Ihr CD-ROM Laufwerk ein.
- Die Autostartfunktion öffnet ein Fenster mit dem Inhalt der CD-ROM.
- Starten Sie die Datei „SETUP.EXE" durch Doppelklick und folgen Sie den Anweisungen, um das Programm und die Medien auf Ihrer Festplatte zu installieren.
- Um das Programm zu installieren, müssen Sie dem Lizenzvertrag zustimmen (s.a. **Lizenz.txt** auf der CD-ROM).
- Den Pfad für die Programminstallation auf der Festplatte können Sie anpassen oder nach der Vorgabe übernehmen.
- Nach Abschluss der Installation können Sie das Programm direkt starten.
- Beim nächsten Aufruf starten Sie das Programm über Ihr Startmenü (Start – Programme – Klett Lehrersoftware – Orange Line – Lehrersoftware Orange Line)

Auf der CD-ROM befindet sich ein ausführliches Handbuch zum Programm.